MY AFRICAN ME

Written By: Ras Jah Strength

Illustrations Rendered By: Makeda Gordon

Dedication

We dedicate this book to all of our beautiful children and grandchildren. We love you so very much.

We would also like to acknowledge all of the beautiful African children of the world. We hope that you are loving yourselves as much as we are loving you.

Note to Parents....

Our prayer is that you will allow this book to be a foundational teaching for you and your children. It is so important that you know who you are and how great you are; but it is even more important that we make sure every

African child knows too.

Introduction

Did you know that all of your beauty comes from inside? The goodness in your heart and your soul is what makes you who you are. You were born with it. Your beauty comes from your **Ancestors**, and they come from Africa.

Did you know that you were from Africa too? Let's learn more about Your African You.

You are a very good person. You are small, but you were smaller before. You are growing and becoming very strong,

forever more.

You think about yourself now. You look at your face in the mirror and know that that is you! You smile and see just how wonderful You are! That's the thing to do.

Look at your eyes, your nose, your lips, they tell you about your family's history and where you come from. There is a good feeling

inside of You, it says "You are welcomed".

Feel your hair, how ticklish it seems. It is having fun on your head curling and curling. It is going this way and that way, playing hide-go-seek, even when you sleep.

Your color of skin is from **melanin**. It is all over you from top to end. A gift that is Great, a beautiful prize, you get light and dark colors, light and dark eyes.

All of this says that you are **African**, a place of sunlight and animals, a beautiful land. **Africa** is the place where everything begins. Where trees becomes trees and wind become wind.

Pangaea was the Earth, it was one complete land. But then it split apart and our portion is African.

BEFORE

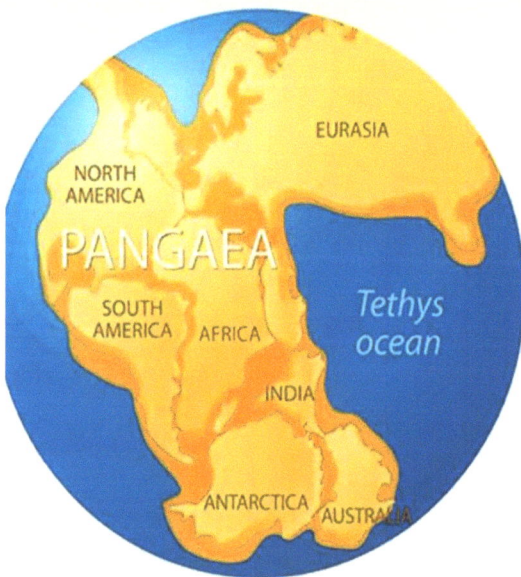

AFTER

Some of our families were on portions that split apart. They look different now-a-days but are still dear to our hearts. They begin to talk a little different and eat different foods, dress in different clothes and wear different shoes. We see them today and think "wow look at your face". But always remember and never forget, we are from the same place.

You are African, that is the name of our land. It was also called **Kemet**, **Alkebu-lan** and **Ethiopian**. **Ethiopia** means that the sun has touched you. That it has kissed your skin to a wonderful hue.

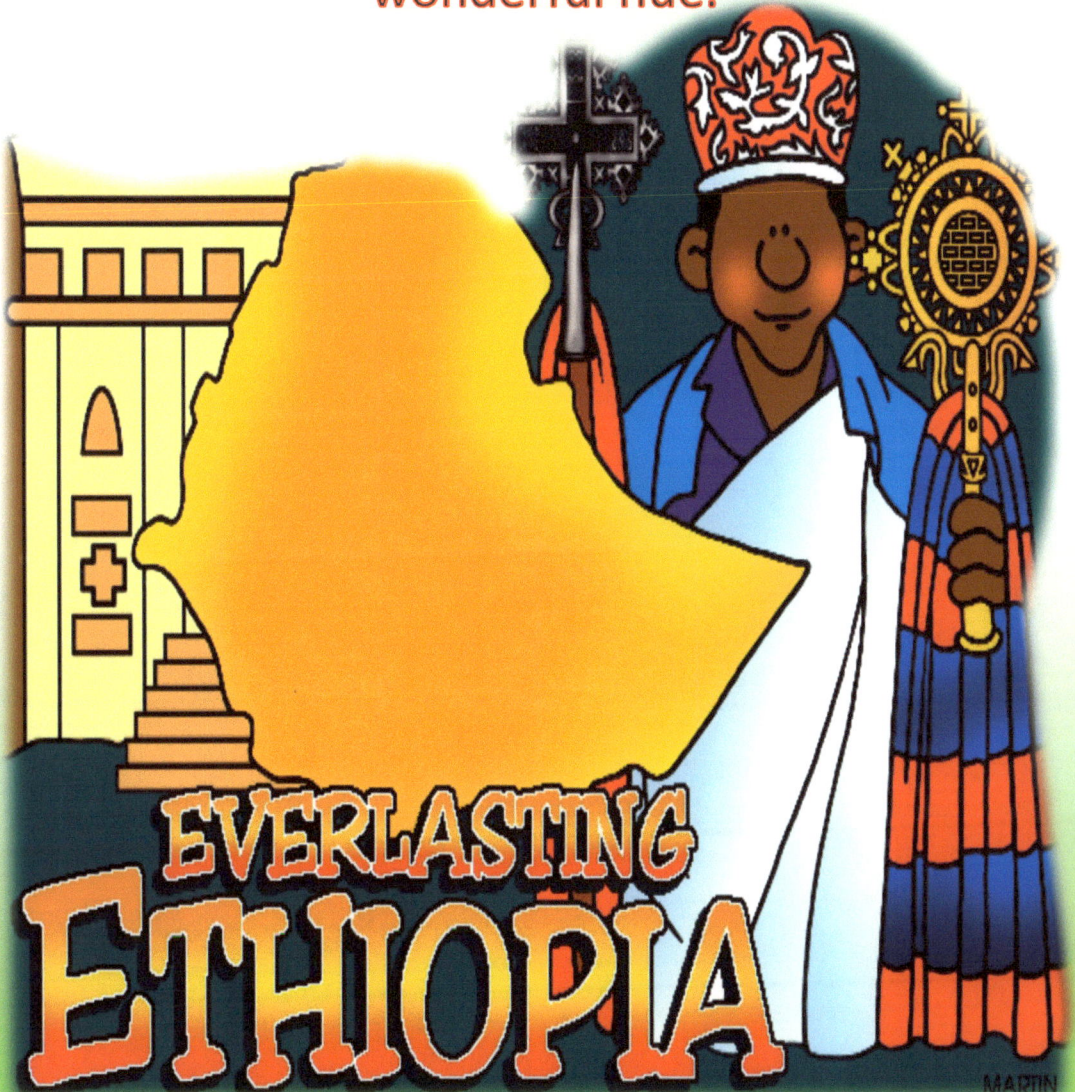

EVERLASTING ETHIOPIA

MARTIN

Being from Africa means that you can stand tall. It means that you can run fast and you can learn all.

Africa is where we started our first school, where we learned about math and science, planting and tools. Africa is where we set our first times, where we drank sweet water, where we saw stars shine. We made the first alphabet. It looked like pictures and stuff. We wrote everything down when we talked about us. We didn't have paper then, so we wrote on stone, you can see the writings now, in the place of our home.

There is something inside of You called **D.N.A**... It is the reason you are living today. **D.N.A** tells your body how it should look. **African D.N.A.** is the oldest in the book.

The first people on earth has the same blood as you do, so all the memory of Africa is inside of you. You are this Beautiful person who will soon begin to show, all of Africa, inside of you, that refulgent glow.

Your arms will become strong and
your feet will become quick. You can
dance and sing, read, count and fix.

You will learn so many things and will remember just how, that's the magic of Africa that's inside of you now. Africa Loves You and wants you to be good. Africa says remember Her, like you know you should.

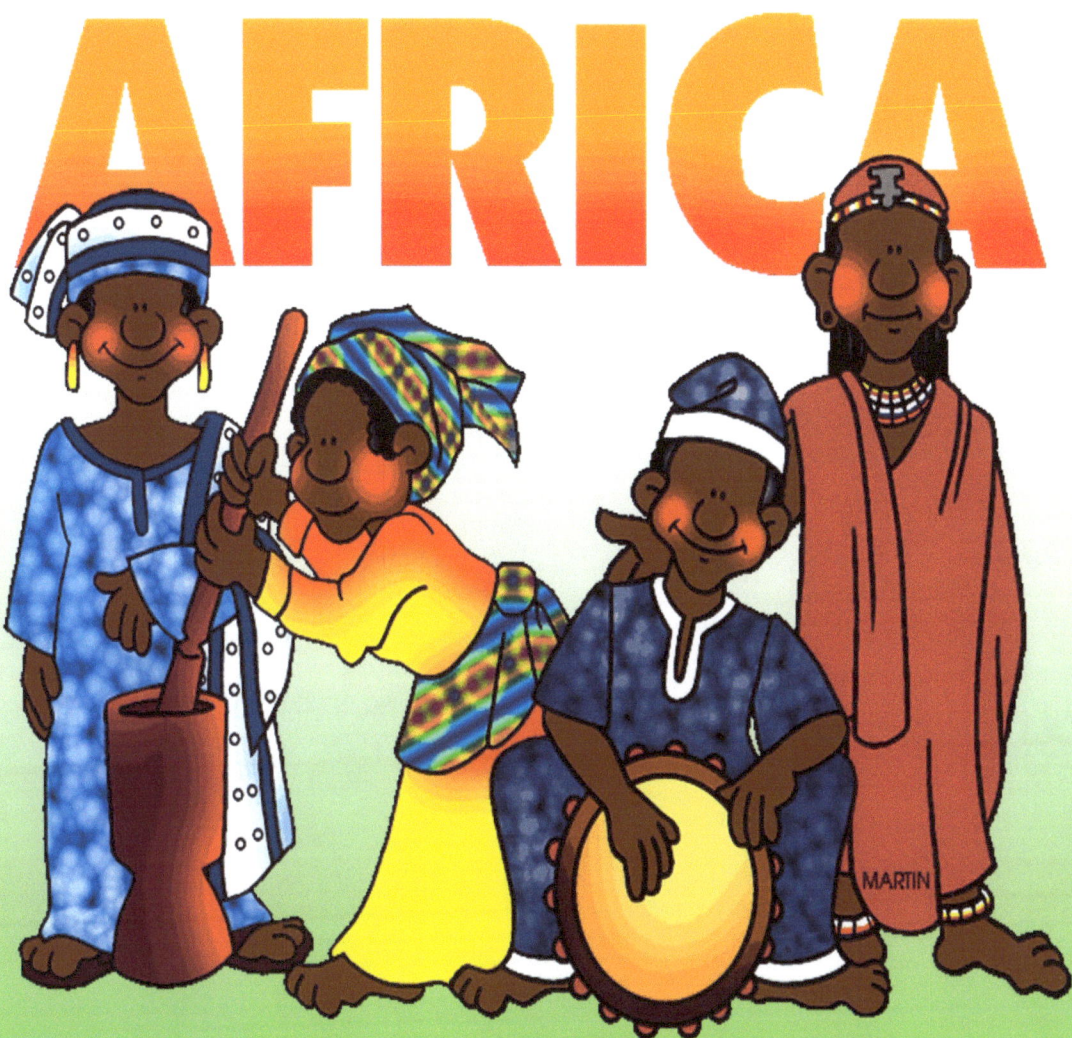

Africa has colors that are beautiful to the mind. They're in the ground and the mountains, the trees and the vines. Colors are also on the animals and birds from ocean to sea.

Africa is most beautiful to see!

Africa gave rise to God, Queens, and Kings,
and spoke to the world the start of these

Beings. Africa says and mention that
angels exist too, not just in books and art but

inside you. In Africa, God's melanin is inside,
not skin, we wear it as a covering to remember

our kin.

<u>Glossary</u>

Melanin: a dark brown to black pigment occurring in the hair, skin, and iris of the eye in people and animals. It is responsible for tanning of skin exposed to sunlight.

African: of or relating to Africa or people of African descent.

Africa: Continents South of Europe and between the Atlantic and Indian Oceans.

Pangaea: is a hypothetical supercontinent that included all current land masses, believed to have been in existence before the continents broke apart during the Triassic and Jurassic Periods.

Alkebu-lan: The ancient name of Africa

Ethiopian: a native or inhabitant of Ethiopia, or a person of Ethiopian descent.

Ethiopia: an ancient region in NE Africa, bordering on Egypt and the Red Sea.

D.N.A.: the fundamental and distinctive characteristics or qualities of someone or something, especially when regarded as unchangeable.

Kemet: the name for Ancient Egypt. It means: "black land", because of the fertile black soils of the Nile flood plains.

Ancestors: a person, typically one more remote than a grandparent, from whom one is descended.

IF YOU ARE INTERESTED IN WRITING AND PUBLISHING WITH SOLOMON & MAKEDA PUBLISHING,

VISIT US AT WWW.SM4PUBLISHING.COM

TODAY AND WE WILL SHOW YOU HOW!

We Love You!